essentials

Oliver D. Doleski

Integrated Business Model

Applying the St. Gallen Management Concept to Business Models

Springer Gabler

Oliver D. Doleski
Munich
Germany

ISSN 2197-6708   ISSN 2197-6716 (electronic)
essentials
ISBN 978-3-658-09697-7   ISBN 978-3-658-09698-4 (eBook)
DOI 10.1007/978-3-658-09698-4

Library of Congress Control Number: 2015940759

Printed on acid-free paper

Springer Fachmedien Wiesbaden is part of Springer Science+Business Media
(www.springer.com)

This 'Essential'

- Presents the conceptual basis of the business model debate
- Introduces a comprehensive approach to business models
- Details the components of the Integrated Business Model
- Provides guidance on business model development

Preface

This volume is based on a chapter of *Smart Market—Vom Smart Grid zum intelligenten Energiemarkt* by Christian Aichele and Oliver D. Doleski, published by Springer Vieweg in 2014. *Smart Market...* is an examination by the two editors and other contributing authors of key areas for action on tomorrow's energy market, in the light of the current debate on Germany's energy transition.

The following pages are a translation of the fully revised and updated version of the chapter by Oliver D. Doleski entitled 'Entwicklung neuer Geschäftsmodelle für die Energiewirtschaft – das Integrierte Geschäftsmodell'. For publication in the 'Springer Essentials' series, the focus of the original article has been changed: this volume takes a broad, cross-sector approach rather than concentrating on the energy market. As well as broadening the proposed business model approach to cover all industries, this volume also modifies and expands each of the five phases of business model development.

Ottobrunn, June 2015   Oliver D. Doleski

Contents

About the author

Oliver D. Doleski is a cross-sector business and process management consultant. He has previously held a number of executive posts in the public sector, and at the German world market leader in the semiconductor sector. Mr. Doleski is currently working on smart markets in the energy industry; the focus of his research is business model development.

Mr. Doleski is actively involved in shaping changes on the German energy market. As editor and author of a wide range of literature in the field, he draws on his expertise and experience in business practice, politics and research.

Introduction

Enterprises throughout the ages have always had to deal with processes of change. The invention of printing with movable type almost wholly superseded the medieval business model of—usually monastic—scriptoria in the space of just a few decades. Change, therefore, is not a modern phenomenon. Yet what is new is the number and growth of influencing factors that now determine business actions. Increasing globalization, more intense competition, ever shorter innovation cycles and growing expectations on the part of stakeholders are just some of the parameters that have a decisive effect on the success of business players.

Change, and increasingly dynamic change, is now more than ever the key factor in management decisions. The complexity arising from this very dynamism is becoming a defining characteristic of today's markets. Traditional methods and business models can deliver less than ideal results in this difficult environment.

Such a situation places the enterprises of today under direct pressure to act. There is now a much greater need for flexibility and innovation, and for effective solutions that fully equip an enterprise to meet political, legal, economic, socio-cultural, technological and ecological challenges.

New approaches to business development are needed. To master complexity, these approaches must fully integrate all of the many and diverse aspects and demands of normative, strategic and operational management. The practical St. Gallen Management Concept offers a good conceptual framework for development: the St. Gallen Concept could be termed the DNA of the Integrated Business Model that is developed and detailed on the following pages.

© Springer Fachmedien Wiesbaden 2015
O. D. Doleski, *Integrated Business Model,* essentials,
DOI 10.1007/978-3-658-09698-4_1

Conceptual Framework and Understanding Business Models

The brief section below outlines the conceptual framework for the sections and chapters that follow. This standard frame of reference should establish a common understanding of the general concept of the business model, before a comprehensive definition of the term is given in Sect. 2.2.

2.1 Origins and Use of the Term 'Business Model'

The term *business model* originated in the information and communications technology (ICT) sector, where it was originally used to map business processes documented as part of the introduction of data processing systems (cf. Kley 2011, p. 1). Literature in the field often links the concept of the business model to the *new economy* of the years 1998 to ca. 2001. However, the term is in fact older, and was already being discussed and applied in business and above all information technology literature even before the emergence of the Internet economy. 'Surprisingly, the query shows that the popularity of the term "business model" is a relatively young phenomenon. Though it appeared for the first time in an academic article in 1957 (Bellman et al. 1957) and in the title and abstract of a paper in 1960 (Jones 1960) [...]' (Osterwalder et al. 2005, p. 6).

The term 'business model' would therefore appear to have emerged not with the new economy, but with the dawning popularity of *business computing* and with the information system architectures of the 1970s and 1980s. Nonetheless, the new economy without a doubt successfully translated to a wider business context a concept that had initially been restricted primarily to the information and communications industry (IC) (cf. Becker et al. 2011, p. 12). However, Porter in particular criticizes the close association between the business model concept and the new economy particularly common in the late 1990s. He believes that the business

© Springer Fachmedien Wiesbaden 2015
O. D. Doleski, *Integrated Business Model*, essentials,
DOI 10.1007/978-3-658-09698-4_2

model should be extended beyond the Internet economy to embrace the economy as a whole, and should above all include the fundamental aspects of strategy and value chain as significant business management factors (cf. Scheer et al. 2003, p. 14). This approach is addressed in more detail in Chap. 3 below.

In the late twentieth and early twenty-first century, therefore, the business model was narrowly understood as a concept for designing information systems. Use of the term has now broadened and it has largely lost its original IC connotation (cf. Stähler 2002, p. 39). Yet despite this significant shift in meaning, a critical look at the applicable literature would still fail to discover a standard definition of the term. So far, there have been numerous and varying views in the field on what specifically the term covers. The popular understanding of the constituent elements of a business model is moreover equally varied, and indeed in some cases contradictory. Such scope and inherent diversity of the 'business model' has so far shaped the academic debate and prevented a common and universal definition of the term.

2.2 Definition of the Business Model

A clear explanation of the business model concept is offered by the etymology of its two constituent words, 'model' and 'business'. Considering these two elements separately offers a better understanding of the content and nature of the concept of the business model.

A *model*[1] is generally understood as a simplified representation of a defined aspect of reality or of the real world. Models always focus on selected and relevant aspects of that reality. A useful model will provide an overview and thus a useful approach to potential solutions to the underlying problem; models are particularly useful for visualizing and structuring complex economic situations (cf. Becker et al. 2012, p. 13). Models can present the real on a large, small or at least simplified scale. They can also—as for example in the fields of business and economics—be wholly abstract in nature. One feature of models worth highlighting is their ability to reduce complexity, and this is discussed in detail in Sect. 3.1.

In the context of business models, the 'model' is the abstract representation of how the business activities of an organization function in reality. Yet what exactly do we mean by 'business'? In principle, *business* can refer to commercial transactions designed to generate revenue and to all operations involving money. In everyday usage, the term can be applied both to the commercial exchange of goods and

---

[1] The word *model* comes from the Latin *modulus* meaning measure, via the Italian *modello* (pattern or draft).

services between business partners (*business* transactions, *business* deals), and the activities of commercial enterprises designed to generate profit (cf. Nemeth 2011, p. 89). 'Business' in a commercial organization can therefore also be understood as covering the structured transformation of input factors into products and services, and the management of interactions with the relevant environment.

If we now combine the implications of 'business' and 'model', this takes us a step closer to understanding the content and nature of a business model. A business model is a simplified, representative description of the following fundamental principle: how an economic system creates value through the transformation of resources and special exchange relationships with other economic entities. A business model, therefore, is a comprehensive, schematic presentation of all of an enterprise's value creation activities and procedures that generate customer value added and long-term revenue. In other words, a business model details an underlying business idea.

As already outlined, literature in the field contains many and in some cases very different definitions of business model. Although the term has been defined many times, a common, precise and universal definition has yet to be established. As the potential scope of the business model is so broad, many authors define the term with a specific focus in mind (cf. Weiner et al. 2010, p. 16). Extensive examinations of the concept have already been published and an explanation of the various definitions will therefore not be undertaken here.

In the absence of a standard definition, the following pages propose a comprehensive, universal definition of the business model that covers all aspects of management. A distinction is drawn between a business model that is not yet to be implemented, which we will refer to as a *business concept*, and an existing business model that is already in place in practice (cf. Stähler 2002, p. 42). However, this distinction is only made in passages where a conscious, methodological differentiation between concept and model is required. In the interests of simplicity, the two terms are otherwise used synonymously.

▷ A **business model** is an applied business concept for describing, analyzing and developing the fundamental procedures underlying business output. A model provides a simplified representation of value creation processes, functions and interactions for creating customer value, securing competitive advantage and generating revenue. A business model is a comprehensive, aggregated picture of reality that can integrate political and legal, economic, socio-cultural, technological and ecological conditions into the transparent architecture required for managing complexity. Alongside normative and strategic parameters, a business model also covers operational and dynamic aspects. The Integrated Business Model ensures that all factors critical to success are considered in full, with clearly defined, structured components.

As the definition proposed here indicates, it is essential for a business model to cover the diverse aspects of production. This point is addressed in detail in Chap. 3 below.

The Integrated Business Model: An Applied Approach

One factor that has defined the world of the twenty-first century is undoubtedly the significant increase in complexity, and this applies equally to all sectors and industries. The introduction in Sect. 3.1 addresses the complexity issue and finds that established business model concepts are in principle suited to reducing complexity, but in practice insufficient in an increasingly difficult environment. A more extensive, comprehensive concept is therefore required for output design. An integrative approach is proposed here as a suitable method for managing complexity in a business context. Before we introduce and detail the idea of the Integrated Business Model, however, Sect. 3.2 outlines the underlying theory: the St. Gallen Management Concept that provides the conceptual basis for the new approach. Section 3.3 outlines the design of the new integrated model and the two sections that follow detail the characteristics and components of that model. If a business model is to be successful in the long term, it cannot be developed or operated in isolation from its environment. Section 3.4 therefore details a method for defining the relevant creative and decision-making scope; Sect. 3.5 then describes the ten core elements of the Integrated Business Model.

3.1 The Business Model: A Tool for Managing Complexity

Growing complexity in almost all areas of the economy is a phenomenon caused by a multitude and variety of influences and environmental factors. Intricacy, diversity and dynamic development are just some of the now common characteristics of the modern business environment. Complexity is in some respects the defining,

© Springer Fachmedien Wiesbaden 2015
O. D. Doleski, *Integrated Business Model*, essentials,
DOI 10.1007/978-3-658-09698-4_3

universal feature to which all market players must adapt their business operations. Any enterprise that ignores the complexity of conditions in its sector or industry does so at its peril. In short, the ability to manage complexity is what distinguishes the successful from the unsuccessful enterprise.

Business Models Are the Right Tool

There is now a greater need than ever for innovative *complexity management* solutions and methods to ensure that enterprise value creation does not become a *complexity trap*. A tried and tested approach to dealing with complexity is to present complex relationships in a structured and abstract form. In economics and in the social sciences, the purpose of models is to reduce complexity to provide a simplified picture of the real world. Models are designed to help deal with complexity. In simple terms, a business model is therefore a complexity management tool (cf. Nemeth 2011, p. 80). The ability of business models to describe business activities as discussed in Sect. 2.2 can enable decision-makers in enterprises to cope with a complex business environment, and to make and implement robust decisions on the basis of the overview provided. In particular, models' inherent ability to translate real phenomena into simplified, realistically structured maps of a section of reality is a great complexity management resource for business practice.

The Limits of Traditional Business Models

In the light of the enormous growth in the complexity and dynamism of modern business environments, enterprises need powerful tools that consider, balance and translate all relevant aspects into a comprehensive solution. Traditional approaches to the business model have in the past proved effective in their various areas of application. However, they sometimes fail to offer the extensive solution required for integrating and examining so many different, complex and often changing conditions. Classic business models generally focus on individual issues and at best a reduction of complexity in isolation. Such approaches do not sufficiently integrate complex conditions and environments effectively to manage complexity. There is often no overarching consideration of relevant influencing factors, with the result that strategic processes do not systematically factor in future issues (cf. Hahn and Prinz 2013, p. 47)—hence the author's attempt here to offer a comprehensive reference model irrespective of sector.

The Principle of Integration

For the management of complexity, we need a central idea; a clear principle on which to shape and design a context-specific model for business activities. The principle of 'integration' with its related concepts of comprehensiveness, uniformity, interconnection and interdisciplinarity is just such an idea.

Challenging conditions and complexity factors in today's economy demand approaches that comprehensively map business activities, and that can therefore flexibly respond to the business environment and to change. New business models must be designed to integrate all relevant aspects into one balanced overall solution. For example, a business model must be able to cover and to link the artifacts strategy, product, market, processes and culture. However, the quality and market suitability of these models does not depend solely on whether they take sufficient account of all influencing factors. Indeed, integration as defined here is also, and perhaps more importantly, the ability effectively to draw on findings and factors from decision theory, economics, engineering, psychology and other disciplines in a comprehensive, interdisciplinary business model.

The benefit of integration as the constitutive principle for developing business models is that such a comprehensive, interdisciplinary approach provides a comprehensive, cross-sector framework for designing viable business models.

3.2 Integrated Management: The Conceptual Basis

As demonstrated above, complexity is a defining aspect of the vast majority of business sectors—and that complexity needs to be managed. Business models have proved a useful tool for reducing and managing complexity in the context of designing and developing approaches to creating value and generating revenue. However, as we have mentioned, traditional models often do not go far enough, in particular in difficult environments; comprehensive, integrated solutions are therefore required.

The Integrated Business Model is presented in detail in Sect. 3.3, but let us look first at the underlying theory. Bleicher's *St. Gallen Management Concept* builds on the systematic approach developed by Hans Ulrich and his students at the University of St. Gallen (cf. Bleicher 2011, p. 85), and offers a useful conceptual framework. Importantly, Bleicher's concept can provide a comprehensive and detailed assessment of many different factors from all areas of management. It is a practice-oriented theory offering a practicable approach to dealing with complex conditions and business environments. In this model, complexity is not simply ignored, nor does application of the simplifying ceteris paribus caveat result in its ultimate removal. Instead, complexity is split up into various different manageable aspects.

Management bodies can use the St. Gallen Management Concept as a form of map for business management guidance, and that is one of the main reasons why it is such a useful frame of reference. The St. Gallen concept does not view enterprises in system-specific isolation; it considers them in relation to and in interaction with relevant environmental conditions. Bleicher's concept also differs from strictly linear cause-and-effect approaches in that it can dynamically integrate the interdependencies and associations found between the various components in real-life business practice with a series of cycles (cf. Bleicher 2011, p. 67).

Three Dimensions of Business Management

All areas of management can be broadly classified in one of *three dimensions* in an approach that distinguishes between the normative, the strategic and the operational level. However, this logical and hierarchical differentiation should not lead to the mistaken assumption that the three dimensions exist in strict isolation. As reflected in the integrated, global understanding of management proposed here, the economic reality is one of numerous relationships and interactions between all three areas. Integrating all three dimensions of business management should therefore be the first step in creating a broader, logical overall concept.

Normative management addresses general business objectives and defines the constitutive values, principles, standards and rules that shape an organization's identity and establish the creative framework for business actions. The normative dimension is always the *basis and justification* for all of an enterprise's activities. A central aspect of normative management is therefore to steer the behavior of the organization and its members with the aim of legitimizing those activities to both external and internal stakeholders.

Strategic management is based on the objectives and rules set by normative management. While normative management justifies business activities, strategic management *steers* those activities. At the strategic level, the focus is on initiatives and projects to be pursued, on the fundamental shape and focus of organizational structures and management systems, and on the problem-solving behavior-shaped by the corporate culture of those at the head of those structures and systems (cf. Bleicher 2003, p. 162).

Practical implementation of normative and strategic tasks is the domain of *operational management*. This, the third dimension of integrated management, is *executive*, i.e. it implements the actions required by the two superordinate dimensions at an operational level. Operational management secures an organization's day-to-day activities.

3.3   iOcTen: A Description of the Integrated Business Model

In Sect. 3.1, we saw that traditional approaches to the business model sometimes deliver less than ideal results in complex business environments. The approach presented below, the 'iOcTen Integrated Business Model ', is therefore designed to integrate all relevant economic aspects and other parameters as we have seen that this integration is required for managing complexity. As outlined, the conceptual frame of reference for iOcTen is the St. Gallen Management Concept.

The key strength of the *Integrated Business Model* lies in the transparent architecture of the model itself. It is integrative and open in structure, and does not from the outset restrict the user to specific businesses, aspects of the value chain, etc. It is a universal approach that comprehensively integrates the demands of normative, strategic and operational management by assigning specific model components to each of these three business management dimensions.

Integrated Business Model Requirements

A successful business model must take account of the entire organization and how it interacts with its environment. Only by integrating all relevant influencing factors and restrictions can a business model lead to processes and ultimately goods and services that pass market testing even in complex environments. A model must also be both universally applicable and designed for intuitive use by managers, business developers and organizational developers. The Integrated Business Model meets all of these requirements, not least because it uses the St. Gallen Management Concept which has a sound theoretical basis and comprehensive structure.

The Five Components of the Integrated Business Model

The Integrated Business Model comprises a total of five structural *components*: the building blocks idea, decision-making scope, model core, development path and success. Fig. 3.1 gives a schematic illustration of the iOcTen structure.

Idea

The development of new business concepts and further development of existing business models always starts with an *idea*. Ideally, the idea should be an initial—

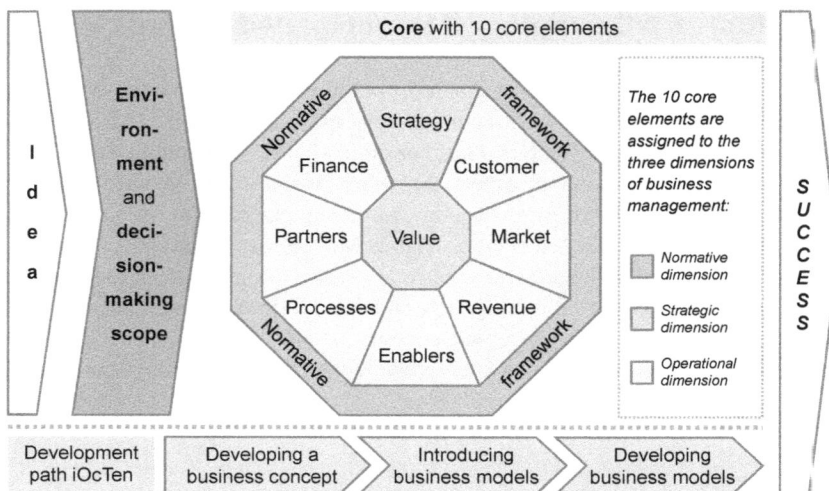

Fig. 3.1 The iOcten integrated business model (schematic diagram)

more than just a vague—concept of what customers on which markets are to be offered the potential products or services.

Environment and Decision-Making Scope

Business activities are always significantly influenced by their *environment*. Environmental factors, general conditions, the demands of relevant stakeholders, etc. define an enterprise's 'creative scope'. The creative scope sets out a range of options that are open to an enterprise and within which that enterprise's management can act. Integrating diverse environmental influences and expectations from relevant stakeholders in this way, the integrated approach is fundamentally open and communication-focused.

Core

The actual business activities of an enterprise are described in the Integrated Business Model using ten constitutive elements that systematically indicate the form of value creation and revenue generation. These ten objects represent the basic, generic building blocks of a business model and can in principle be found in all models irrespective of sector or application. Altogether, these ten elements form the *core* of the Integrated Business Model.

All elements in the core together cover the normative, strategic and operational dimensions of management, linking the business model core to the St. Gallen Management Concept. The first element, *normative framework*, represents the normative dimension and the two elements *value* and *strategy* the strategic dimension of a business model. The elements *customer*, *market*, *revenue*, *enablers*, *processes*, *partners* and *finance* are part of the operational dimension of the Integrated Business Model.

The ten elements in the integrated model cannot be structured solely on the basis of the three dimensions of business management discussed above. Drawing on Stähler's business model definition, we can distinguish a number of key questions relating to three areas (levels) in total, which are proposed here as an additional structural classification tool:

- **Value proposition level (value proposition)**
  What is the enterprise offering its customers and partners? *What value* is it creating?
- **Source of revenue level (revenue generation)**
  Who is demanding products and services and why? *By what means* can sustainable yield be generated?
- **Value creation level (value creation)**
  How is output generated? (cf. Stähler 2002, p. 41 f.).

In a similar classification to the fields of management, the *normative framework*, *value* and *strategy* elements are part of the *what*. The elements *customer*, *market* and *revenue* come under *who* or *by what means,* and the elements *enablers*, *processes*, *partners* and *finance* under *how*. These classification criteria produce a two-dimensional matrix which is illustrated by Table 3.1 and Fig. 3.2.

The core of the Integrated Business Model is a regular octagon with a border, a middle section and a central element. The business model name *iOcTen* comes from the choice of illustration: in the integrated (**i**) model proposed here, the octagon (**Oc**) groups eight of the ten (**Ten**) core elements around the *value* in the center and within the *normative framework* element around the edge. Although the term iOcTen strictly speaking only refers to the octagonal model, this name is used below as a synonym for the entire Integrated Business Model.

A special position in the iOcTen model core is occupied by the *normative framework* element, which surrounds the other nine core elements. This element of

Table 3.1 Dimensions, levels and elements of the iOcTen Integrated Business Model (overview)

	Normative dimension (justification)	Strategic dimension (steering)	Operational dimension (execution)
Value proposition level (What? What value?)	[1] Normative framework	[2] Value [3] Strategy	
Source of revenue level (By what means? Who?)			[4] Customer [5] Market [6] Revenue
Value creation level (How?)			[7] Enablers [8] Processes [9] Partners [10] Finance

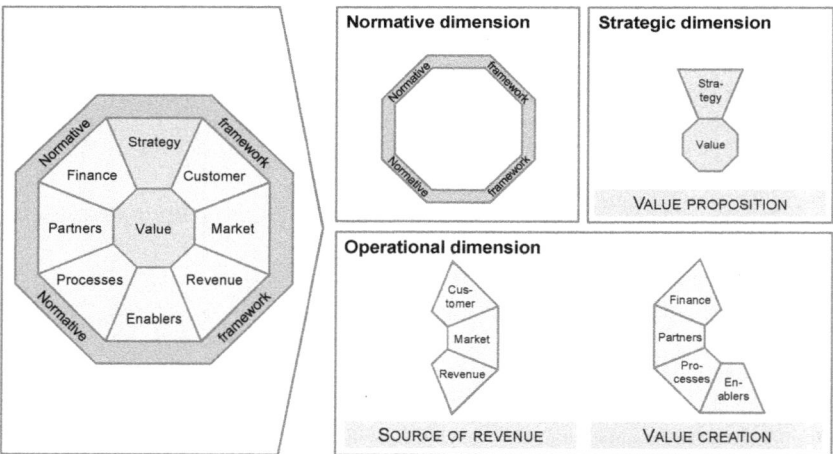

Fig. 3.2 Dimensions and thematic levels of the model core

the model brings the diverse parameters from the upstream *decision-making scope* component into the center of the model. The *normative framework* therefore has a transfer and filter function between the external organizational environment on the one hand and the internal aspects on the other.

At the very center of the octagonal core of iOcTen is the *value* element and that is no coincidence. Positioning this element in the middle demonstrates the enormous significance of the *value proposition* as a central aspect of any business model. Moreover, like the *normative framework*, the value component and its interactions influence the remaining elements of the core so that here too, the central position reflects a great interdependency with the remaining elements. The position is designed to express the enormous overall importance of the value proposition to business success. By highlighting value, iOcTen differs significantly from the popular Business Model Canvas by Osterwalder and Pigneur. The Business Model Canvas puts the customers at the center of every business model (cf. Osterwalder and Pigneur 2011, p. 24). At the center of iOcTen, on the other hand, is always the value that customers and partners can obtain from an enterprise's business activities.

The Development Path

Modeling and structured development of business models is a key area of business action. The iOcTen Integrated Business Model therefore does not focus solely on comprehensively integrating the ten individual aspects outlined into the overall model. Integrating a *development path* as a dynamic factor in the model is equally important. Chap. 4 describes in detail the three stages of this *development path*: *concept development*, *implementation* and *further development*.

Success

Success is the last of the total of five components of iOcTen and represents the result of business activities. Success is therefore a measure of the output of the business model/business activities.

3.4   Environment: The Basis of Business Actions—The Decision-Making Scope

Before an idea becomes a specific business model, knowledge of the relevant parameters and conditions is needed to establish the fundamental potential creative scope for a business project. As business activities cannot, in practice, develop in isolation from the structure of their environment, there should be a focus on analyzing the essential environmental conditions even before the content of a business model is defined. Porter emphasizes the link between the business model on the one hand and the environment on the other as follows: '[…] no business model can be evaluated independently of industry structure' (Porter 2001, p. 73). The way in which an organization interacts with its environment is a major factor in the success or failure of business models. As an open system that interacts with its environment through many different relationships, an enterprise can only survive if it pays sufficient attention to environmental conditions in both the design and the implementation of a business model (cf. Bergmann and Bungert 2011, p. 26).

Environment has a significant influence on the design of business models. One interesting question in this context, however, would be whether the given environment is to be seen as absolutely fixed, or whether in fact the actions of individual enterprises can, to a certain extent, shape their environments. The strictly *deterministic approach* would be that an enterprise must accept all environmental parameters as fixed and beyond its sphere of influence. This view of a fixed, restricted scope for organizations is however not the approach taken here. Numerous examples of innovative business models from recent years prove that environmental conditions are not absolute determinants of the behavior of economic entities (cf. Bornemann 2010, p. 50 f.). Agile enterprises that set the right strategic focus are able actively to change certain environmental conditions and to position themselves within their environment (cf. Bornemann 2010, p. 53). Qualifying the strictly deterministic approach in this way is useful for business model design and development, as it overcomes limits and restrictions, either potential or merely imagined, and reduces obstacles posed by the specific environment. Ultimately, this makes it possible to develop completely new business models.

Decision-Making Scope: The Context for Business Model Development

The business environment with its many and diverse aspects and conditions is an external factor. Together with an enterprise's internal management goals and the critical factors for success specific to an organization, this external factor defines the *creative scope* within which a business model can be designed or improved. Where decision theory traditionally employs the term 'field of decision', iOcTen uses the clearer, more illustrative concept of *decision-making scope*. The decision-making scope crystallizes the potential options and alternatives for action in a business model.

The decision-making scope consists of scope for action, which can be directly influenced by decision-makers, and a fixed scope, which cannot. As that part of the decision-making scope that can be influenced, the *scope for action* represents the sum of all alternatives for action that are in principle possible, and which management weighs against the target system of the organization to find the set of options promising maximum value. The *fixed scope*, on the other hand, covers all relevant environmental parameters and circumstances over which the enterprise has no direct control. The parameters of this scope represent rigid, unchangeable data or circumstances for the decision-makers, hence the term fixed.

To return to the deterministic approach to business environments, it is worth noting that the content of the fixed scope should by no means limit creativity in the design and development of business models, or indeed predetermine in absolute terms the end result. The environment should, however, shape the content of design to produce sensible, viable decisions. With a pioneering or indeed revolutionary idea, the management of an enterprise can in fact ultimately also influence its external environment—a new, innovative business model can put the enterprise at the forefront of development and set new standards (cf. Osterwalder and Pigneur 2011, p. 204). This is an important point, and underlines the need to move away from a rigidly deterministic approach to the business environment.

Developing Recommendations: Exploring the Decision-Making Scope

The decision-making scope in the iOcTen Integrated Business Model is an outline, guide and a range of alternatives. Within this scope, management can develop and define genuine options by assessing objectives and related performance, and the various factors for success. Recommendations on this basis are integrated into the business model core through the normative core component of the *normative framework*.

The procedure proposed below is an appropriate tool both for designing completely new business models and for developing existing ones. The basic options possible with business models are established following a multi-stage procedure which is illustrated in the schematic diagram in Fig. 3.3 and is as follows:

Step 1 Comparison of objectives and performance. The management starts by establishing the organization's current situation. This is done by checking business objectives against progress on those objectives to date.

Step 2 Assessment of the environment. Once the decision-makers have a clear picture of their enterprise's performance, they also need a reliable overview of the relevant business model environment. Important environmental aspects are the political and legal framework, society and relevant stakeholders, the macroeconomy, the market, technology, ecology, resources, and trends. Management can start its assessment of the decision-making scope by focusing purely on exploring and establishing these environmental aspects. When and if the options established on the basis of the decision-making scope clearly indicate potential for implementa-

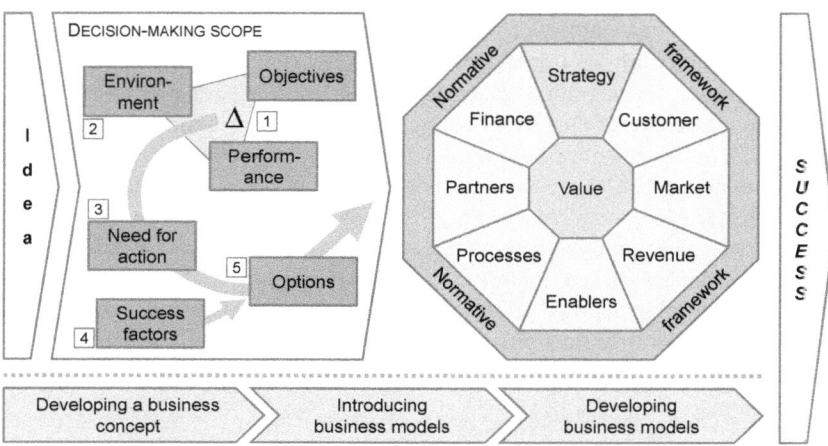

Fig. 3.3 iOcTen Integrated Business Model (with focus on decision-making scope)

tion of a business idea, this initial step is then followed by a detailed analysis using the ten core elements of the iOcTen Integrated Business Model.

Step 3 Establishing the need for action. Once the environment has been analyzed, the need for action is defined in both qualitative and quantitative terms. The three-sided analysis presents and compares objectives, performance and the environment. Progress on objectives is compared with the relevant environmental factors; this assessment provides a picture of what measures or actions are required for achieving the objectives of the business model in the light of the environmental conditions.

Step 4 Establishing success factors and checking relevance. To develop specific options from the established need for action, we first need to establish the critical success factors and evaluate their relevance to the business model. Success factors represent aspects of business and the business environment that play a major role in the success of an organization or business model.

Step 5 Defining options. Success factors complement the 'need for action' already established management defines genuine options by comparing and contrasting the two. An enterprise asks itself two key questions: firstly, what is required to achieve the objective (need for action), and secondly, what specific resources can it employ to make its business model work (success factors). The answers to these two questions define the options for business action (options).

Step 6 Setting recommendations. A final recommendation is drawn up on the basis of the options defined. This recommendation is to an extent integrated into the core of the business model through the *normative framework* element. If the original idea for a business model is found not to meet the requirements of the decision-making scope, the business model is abandoned or completely revised at this point. The business model approach pursued up until this point would in such a case be abandoned.

3.5   Elements of the Integrated Business Model

Section 3.3 outlined the general concept of the iOcTen Integrated Business Model. The following chapter now focuses in detail on the content and contribution of the ten elements of the *core* component. By describing and analyzing the individual core elements of the Integrated Business Model, the following pages should create a common understanding of the internal structure of iOcTen and how it operates.

Table 3.2 clearly illustrates how each of the ten elements of the core of the business model relates to the normative, strategic and operational spheres of management. The table also lists a number of synonyms used in the relevant literature and provides examples of areas for action in business practice and the core elements to which they correspond.

Normative Framework

The first of the ten core elements is the *normative framework*, which represents the *normative dimension* of the business model. This element has two main functions in iOcTen: firstly, it inputs the results of the decision-making scope, and consequently the influence of the business environment, into the business model and ultimately into the core of the business model. The normative framework is also the scope within which an organization defines basic parameters and general, long-term business model objectives.

In iOcTen, the normative element surrounds the other nine elements of the core. The normative aspect influences all of these elements equally, transferring the various influencing parameters from the upstream *decision-making scope* component to the core of the model. Systematically considering normative environmental conditions in this way integrates essential external data and restrictions into the business model, and consequently ensures the stability and long-term viability of the model itself. At the same time, addressing at an early stage the defining environmental conditions and their effect on potential products and services is designed to

Table 3.2 Categorization of content and synonyms by core element of the iOcTen Integrated Business Model (selection). (Source: Author's research)

Element	Dimension	Synonyms (literature)	Content (selection)
[1] Normative framework	Normative	Standards	Corporate philosophy
			Business objectives/purpose
			Internal legal structure
			Business policy
			Corporate culture
[2] Value	Strategic	Value proposition, Value dimension	Customer requirements
			Output
			Value
[3] Strategy	Strategic	Strategy model, Strategy area	Strategic objectives and scope
			Management
			Problem-solving
			Organizational structures
[4] Customer	Operational	Customer dimension, Customer model, Customer concept, Customer focus	Customer segment
			Distribution channels
			Customer relationships
			Value communication
[5] Market	Operational	Market proposition model	Market structure
			Market segmentation
			Competitors
[6] Revenue	Operational	Value capture, Sales, Profit model, Revenue model	Revenue strategies
			Pricing policy
			Price strategy
			Pricing
[7] Enablers	Operational	Resources, Resource model, Enablers	Human resources
			Knowledge/expertise
			Skills
			Intangible resources
			Tangible resources
[8] Processes	Operational	Value creation, Value creation concept	Value creation
			Value chain
			Value chain configuration
[9] Partners	Operational	Value constellation, Network, Network model	Partners
			Partner channels
			Partner relationships
			Value transfer
[10] Finance	Operational	Finance model, Capital model, Cost	Finance
			Sources/forms of finance
			Cost structure
			Value dissemination

minimize the serious danger of poor decision-making and errors in planning. If the original idea behind a business model and implementation of that idea prove wholly or partly unworkable in the light of environment considerations, the iOcTen *normative framework* can halt the development of unrealistic, non-viable approaches at a very early stage. The model thus prevents the risk of spiraling non-value costs in business model development.

In the context of developing existing business models, the *normative framework* also defines all objectives that the business model is pursuing, and comprehensively integrates into the model all business parameters designed to secure the enterprise's long-term survival and development capabilities. An enterprise must ensure viability by securing its business model identity in the social and economic environment; this is the main driver behind strategic development of the competitive skills that are a prerequisite for positive development (cf. Bleicher 2003, p. 161).

In this central transfer and filter function between the external organizational environment and the internal enterprise environment, the normative framework determines both the content and the specific form and focus of constitutive aspects of the business model: general objectives, standards, principles, ideals, ground rules, values, business ethics, corporate culture, internal legal structure, business policy, business purpose, legal aspects, etc.

Value

Market trends across all industries over recent years clearly show that products and services on the markets of the future will generally only be successful if based on sound, stable business models and also offer their users key value (cf. Bühner et al. 2012, p. 5). In other words, enterprises will, as a rule, only prosper with their business models if their products and customer solutions create *value* at market conditions. On the ever-competitive market, successful enterprises are those which continue to discover value-adding opportunities and to use these more effectively than their competitors, i.e. with greater value (cf. Rüegg-Stürm 2004, p. 69).

Considering the great significance of value creation to the economic survival of enterprises and their business models, the value element and the *strategy* element together represent the *strategic dimension* of iOcTen. Assigning value to the strategic level of the business model is hardly a surprising approach if we consider that customers are only interested in a product or service if they believe that it will offer them value. Value is also a key factor that distinguishes an enterprise from its competitors. Each and every business model should therefore include a description of the product or service that clearly details its value for the customer (cf. Zolnowski and Böhmann 2010, p. 32). That is why the value proposition has a central role in iOcTen, illustrated by the central position of the *value* element in the central octagon. Like the *normative framework*, value also influences the other elements in the core of the model.

For business models to create value, their products and services must be designed or developed to offer the best possible response to customers' and business partners' requirements. Far-reaching decisions must therefore be taken by the management on what specific needs and demands a business model is to fulfill. Management can draw on a range of value categories to make the right decision in any given situation. Osterwalder and Pigneur cite categories such as design, brand and status, price, cost reductions, risk minimization, availability and convenience/ usability (cf. Osterwalder and Pigneur 2011, p. 28 f.). A number of other value aspects are also of relevance to the Integrated Business Model alongside the examples given here. These could perhaps be termed as 'soft' value aspects: aspects that are subjectively perceived by the recipients as more or less real benefits.

After responding in detail to the question of what specific needs and demands a business model is to cover, management has a firm, reliable idea of what products or services to market or continue to market, and in what configuration and customer segment, in order to create value.

Strategy

Strategic goals, scope, management, problem-solving, organizational structure, etc. form the *Strategy* element in the iOcTen Integrated Business Model. A detailed observation of these aspects should create the right framework for operational management to implement in practice the normative requirements defined in the *normative framework*. To this end, decisions must be taken in strategic management to define the future and objectives of the product or service, decisions that have implications far beyond short-term, day-to-day business (cf. Zolnowski and Böhmann 2010, p. 33).

The main aspect of *strategy* is ensuring that a business model creates long-term competitive advantages, even and above all in a complex market environment, and ultimately ensures the future viability of the organization. One of the primary functions of strategic management and the strategy element of iOcTen is to create and develop long-term potential. This is done with a set of strategies and procedures that directly affect both the market position and internal resource base—both external and internal business model factors. Strategic management establishes a long-term framework and guide for defining the content of the seven remaining core operational elements. *Strategy* and the *normative framework* thus together provide the strategic focus both for the enterprise and for each and every business model (cf. Bergmann and Bungert 2011, p. 25).

Customer

Who will pay for the product or service provided? The answer to this simple question is generally equally simple: the customer! No one would seriously dispute the fact that even the best business model in theory is wholly worthless without customers who are willing to pay. *Customer* is therefore a significant element of the iOcTen Integrated Business Model. In fact, the role of the customer is so important to the success of enterprises and their business models that literature in the field often puts the customer at the very center. Osterwalder and Pigneur, for example, argue that as a business model will not survive for long on the market without profitable customers, customers comprise the heart of any business model (cf. Osterwalder and Pigneur 2011, p. 24). Whilst customers are also of great significance in iOcTen, the heart of the Integrated Business Model is in fact the value that the model offers customers and partners.

At the center of the *customer* element are the needs and demands of those players at which an enterprise is targeting its products and services. A detailed understanding of the relevant customers and partners is essential when developing new business concepts or existing business models: the business model must be tailored to those customers' and partners' wishes, ideas, specifications, etc. The better an enterprise understands and responds to the needs of its primary target group, the customers, the more successful its models will be on the market.

There is no one, single, generic customer. 'Customers' usually covers many, and in some cases very different, individuals or organizations, whom or which cannot be targeted and served individually. Customers are therefore assigned to separate, clearly defined segments that structure and categorize all customers on the basis of set criteria. *Customer segments* allow an enterprise's management to make a conscious choice of segments to cater for and segments to ignore. Once this decision is made, a business model can be carefully designed around an in-depth understanding of the target customers' needs (cf. Osterwalder and Pigneur 2011, p. 24).

Customer segmentation is the basis for analyzing and defining the *customer relationship* that an enterprise or business model is to develop and maintain with the selected groups of customers. A business model will only be a market success if it can attract customers willing to pay for its products or services, and build up long-term loyalty to the company. Customer relationship management is therefore a key function, but one that comes at a cost. 'All customer interactions between a firm and its clients affect the strength of the relationship a company builds with its customers. But as interactions come at a given cost, firms must carefully define what kind of relationship they want to establish with what kind of customer' (Osterwalder 2004, p. 71). In the light of this cost issue, one of the main tasks is selecting and shaping the method of customer acquisition and retention. At the business development stage, the enterprise must decide whether to focus on personal assistance, dedicated personal assistance, self-service, automated services over the Internet, etc.

Market

The *market* element of the business model is a detailed analysis of market structure and competition. The findings of this analysis together with information from other iOcTen modules are used to develop suitable product-market combinations, and also help to create appropriate channels of interaction between enterprises and their customers.

In-depth knowledge of key market characteristics and an exact picture of the structure of the business model environment are essential if an enterprise is to recognize market opportunities and integrate them as rapidly as possible into new business models. Other important parameters in business model design are the needs and demands of the various stakeholders in terms of product and service features.

Where *market structure* focuses mainly on the environment of a business model, *competition* concentrates on the—usually rival—players operating on the relevant markets. In this contest, an enterprise must be able to respond to tactical maneuvers by its competitors and to launch countermeasures to ensure the economic survival of its own business model (cf. Wirtz 2011, p. 138).

An analysis of market data establishes the defining market factors for business model design. *Market analysis* is typically conducted in three stages:

1. Check whether there is access to a sufficient quantity and quality of resources for business model implementation (procurement market structure).
2. Apply the findings of the competitive environment analysis to the customer structure established in the *customer* component (sales market structure).
3. Anticipate the potential legal risks associated with the introduction of the business model, for example breach of commercial property rights, liability, legal requirements (legal framework) (cf. Wirtz 2011, p. 139 f.).

Revenue

In a market economy, enterprises are constantly seeking maximum profit for capital invested, i.e. the maximal possible return on equity and loan capital. This phenomenon, which Gutenberg calls the *profit principle* [*erwerbswirtschaftliches Prinzip*], is represented in the Integrated Business Model by the core element *revenue* (cf. Gutenberg 1990, p. 43).

Setting aside exceptional situations in which high-loss business models are artificially maintained for image or similar reasons, a business model can only contribute to an enterprise's long-term success if it generates reasonable profits in line with Gutenberg's principle. But how does an enterprise generate the necessary revenue from its business model in practice? In response to this central question for business model development, the *revenue* element in iOcTen contains a description of sources and procedures from and by which the enterprise generates its income, giving a detailed insight into the revenue mechanisms underlying the business model (cf. Stähler 2002, p. 47).

In principle, revenue can come from *one-off, transactional payments* or from *regular payments* which are not in direct return for supply or provision by the enterprise—for example payments for rights of use, service, basic charges, etc. The most common sources of revenue include the direct sale of products and services, the issue of rights (licenses), the collection of fees, the hire of assets and external publicity funding.

Once suitable sources of revenue for the business concept or business model have been identified, the overall *revenue mechanism* for the business model is then developed. The revenue mechanism links the relevant selection of revenue sources with pricing methods based on suitable *price models* for each situation. The *pricing mechanism* sets an individual price for each product or service based on factors such as costs, expected profitability, fixed market and strategic parameters, etc. The creative role of the decision-makers is not limited to setting staggered and absolute prices. Also and more importantly, they must decide whether the products and services in a business model are to be marketed at fixed, variable or semi-variable prices.

Enablers

Enablers are all major input factors or resources that enable the actual implementation of business models. These elements make it possible for the enterprise to offer a product or service, and therefore to supply a business model's target markets

Table 3.3 Categories of business model enablers (selection). (Source: Author's research)

Human	Physical	Intellectual	Financial
Managers	Land	Skills	Funding
Staff	Buildings	Knowledge/expertise	Securities
Management processes	Machinery	R&D	Credit facilities
Trust	Tools	Patents/rights	…
…	Transport facilities	Copyrights	
	Vehicles	Brands	
	Warehouses	Image	
	Technology	Information	
	Infrastructure	Data	
	Systems/networks	Quality management	
	…	…	

(cf. Zolnowski and Böhmann 2010, p. 32). Osterwalder and Pigneur believe that enablers can be both internal and external factors from an enterprise's perspective, and that they can be human, physical, intellectual or financial (cf. Osterwalder and Pigneur 2011, p. 38). Table 3.3 sets out a selection of key *enablers*.

Management should always focus on those enablers that competitors cannot emulate, or can only emulate with difficulty. Examples of such enablers include unusual expertise, specific process knowledge, long-term patents, corporate image and a strong brand. Integrating these important and difficult to emulate resources into a business model can offer a significant, long-term competitive advantage. Management should therefore design business models to include as many of these hard or impossible-to-imitate aspects as possible (cf. Wirtz 2011, p. 130).

Processes

The *processes* element can be used to analyze, optimize and document all activities in the Integrated Business Model that directly or indirectly contribute to output and therefore create value. In other words, this core element allows a detailed analysis and description of those processes and activities that, as it were, bring a business model to life and provide the framework for generating revenue in accordance with the profit principle.

The *business processes* that determine the business model must always be designed to deliver the output that best meets the needs of customers and business partners.

Partners

Under pressure from strong trends such as increasing globalization, tougher competition, greater customization, demographic change and technological progress, enterprises must respond by developing skills for the future as they often do not have all of the necessary competencies. Partnerships are a useful option here as they can allow enterprises significantly to extend the limited scope for action determined by their available expertise and limited resources.

The purpose of the core element *partners* in the Integrated Business Model is the creation of customer value through optional cooperation by suppliers and partners within a network. In the case of complex products and services in particular, partnerships help to extend the portfolio available and therefore sustainably to improve business models. Often, forms of collective production and output can be absolutely essential to a functioning business. Dividing value creation between the various members of a network can significantly improve what are, when considered in isolation, the limited options of the individual participating organizations. Partnerships also reduce the risks attached to a business model, offer scale benefits in procurement, and considerably extend the available resource base for each member of the network.

A key benefit of the *partners* element in iOcTen is the opportunity systematically to assess the de facto quantitative and qualitative contribution of network partners to total value creation and thus to the business model. *Partners*, together with the *process* element to which it is closely linked, provides an analysis of data streams and the flow of goods and services, giving management a picture of how individual partners contribute to the business model in practice and what their contribution is actually worth. It should be noted that the issue of fairly balancing and reconciling partner interests is particularly relevant in the context of return on capital. The success of a partnership is largely dependent on how the revenue from a business model is distributed amongst the network participants. If a network of partners is to be effective in the long term, a modus vivendi must be found that guarantees each partner a share of revenue commensurate with that partner's individual contribution to value creation, and that therefore positively contributes to partners' return on capital. Suitable rules and procedures should be drafted and agreed that allow potential synergy and efficiency improvements to be harnessed, and a fair balance of and recompense for value obtained and provided. Indeed, such rules could go as far as defining payment obligations for the various value creation partners (cf. Bach et al. 2003, p. 12).

Working in collective network structures also achieves the reduction in complexity advocated here, by allowing partners to focus their activities on core competencies that offer better value to stakeholders and the opportunity to build up a successful, strategic market position (cf. Bleicher 2003, p. 149). For the sake of completeness, we should however note that business models are only accepted by customers if the complexity of the network does not affect their relationship with the principal. Ultimately, a customer will always expect a reduction in complexity, and this must be guaranteed with a single, consistent public presence and clearly defined customer interfaces (cf. Bach 2003, p. 342).

Notwithstanding the many benefits of value creation in partnership listed above, network-based business models do also have potential disadvantages which cannot be ignored. Partnerships do not only extend the sphere of action and increase the strategic flexibility and power of all participating organizations, they also intensify any problems faced by those organizations' management bodies. Before entering a network, each individual enterprise is governed solely by its own executive. In a network, problems require a consensus from all business partners, who may be operating in very different conditions and situations (cf. Bleicher 2003, p. 148). Business model design must therefore also focus on aspects such as the structure of inter-organizational cooperation, managing critical interfaces between value creation partners, and a fair and appropriate balancing of the various partners' interests.

Finance

The *finance* element combines the two aspects of funding and cost or cost structure of a business model. It maps the method of financing for the business model and analyzes the cost structure. An assessment of the relevant monetary parameters of a business model is required as this point, and to avoid underfunding and escalating costs, such an assessment must always take account of both normative and strategic factors. *Finance* is also closely linked to *revenue*: a business model's margin can be calculated directly from the ratio of revenue on the one hand to costs on the other.

As we have already seen, the finance component comprises funding and cost structure. *Funding* assesses and defines the absolute financial resources of a business model, and plans possible refinancing or capital procurement. Funding also covers the examination and assessment of a business model's financial success using financial data from previous periods; this data is also used to forecast funding and liquidity requirements. Overall, the funding aspect produces short-term, medium-term and long-term financial planning for each business model (cf. Wirtz 2011, p. 153).

The *cost structure* of a business model indicates what costs will result from which activities in the course of value creation, and how high those costs will be. *Cost structure analysis* is used to assess the feasibility of business models using cost/quantity functions. Each activity that contributes to business model implementation is first directly allocated the costs incurred. For existing business models, this is done by analyzing historical data, and for planned business concepts by extrapolating suitable benchmarks. The second step is to assess, through appropriate comparisons, the cost efficiency of the cost factors established. Each business model is then analyzed for relevant cost drivers on the basis of these findings. Cost structure analysis for each business model can identify potential savings and help to establish specific cost reduction measures. If the analysis uncovers unacceptable costs, product or service development can be adapted or indeed even abandoned at the planning stage of the business model before any actual outflow of liquidity.

The Three Stages of Business Model Development

The three stages of *business model development* represent the dynamic element of the iOcTen Integrated Business Model. These stages and the subordinate idea, analysis, design, implementation and improvement phases are systematically assigned to the ten elements of the business model core as outlined in Sect. 3.5.

Using the ten elements of the model core, management can develop a structured design and selection process for potential business models at a very early stage. Complete and systematic allocation of all business content to the various phases of development minimizes the risk of important content being forgotten, and of seemingly unimportant aspects carelessly being ignored in business model design. Carefully considering the comprehensive set of criteria for all ten elements also obviates the need to run through the entire *business concept development* process: the structured procedure flags up possible weaknesses. In such cases, the entrepreneur should consider appropriate exit strategies if the major weaknesses in the business model idea cannot be eliminated in the course of this process (cf. Wirtz 2011, p. 233). Incidentally, this structured design and selection process is one of the key strengths of the iOcTen Integrated Business Model.

A distinction is generally drawn between two main uses for business models. Business models can be developed for implementing completely new business ideas, or what is for the enterprise in question a new business. The business model design process can also be applied to further develop an existing, established business. As shown in the schematic diagram in Fig. 4.1, the former case covers the two stages of development *business concept development* and *business model introduction*; in the latter case, the focus is on the continued evolution of existing models.

As we are distinguishing here between new business models that are yet to be implemented, and established business models, we will return to the distinction drawn in the definitions section above between business concept and busi-

© Springer Fachmedien Wiesbaden 2015
O. D. Doleski, *Integrated Business Model,* essentials,
DOI 10.1007/978-3-658-09698-4_4

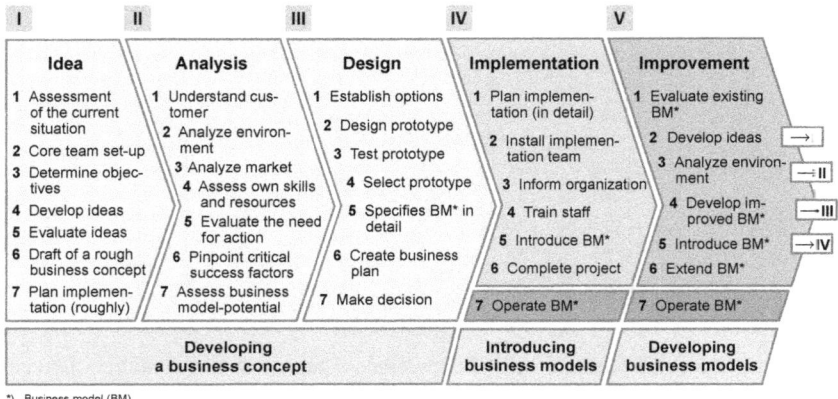

I	II	III	IV	V
Idea	**Analysis**	**Design**	**Implementation**	**Improvement**
1 Assessment of the current situation	1 Understand customer	1 Establish options	1 Plan implementation (in detail)	1 Evaluate existing BM*
2 Core team set-up	2 Analyze environment	2 Design prototype	2 Install implementation team	2 Develop ideas
3 Determine objectives	3 Analyze market	3 Test prototype	3 Inform organization	3 Analyze environment
4 Develop ideas	4 Assess own skills and resources	4 Select prototype	4 Train staff	4 Develop improved BM*
5 Evaluate ideas	5 Evaluate the need for action	5 Specifies BM* in detail	5 Introduce BM*	5 Introduce BM*
6 Draft of a rough business concept	6 Pinpoint critical success factors	6 Create business plan	6 Complete project	6 Extend BM*
7 Plan implementation (roughly)	7 Assess business model-potential	7 Make decision	7 Operate BM*	7 Operate BM*
	Developing a business concept		**Introducing business models**	**Developing business models**

*) Business model (BM)

Fig. 4.1 Development path in the iOcTen Integrated Business Model

ness model. Section 4.1 below details the modeling of business models yet to be implemented, and therefore uses the term business concept. Section 4.2 outlines the introduction of a business concept in practice, closely connected to modeling, and therefore uses the term business model. Section 4.3 then examines the further development of existing business models.

4.1   Developing a Business Concept

The first stage of business model development is to *draft the business concept.* This part of the business model *development path* can in turn be divided into three phases: idea, analysis and design. In practice, these phases and all the activities that they involve are seldom completed in such a strict order as this list would suggest. Many activities belonging to the analysis and design phase are in fact conducted simultaneously for practical reasons.

Phase I: Idea

In the case of established enterprises in particular, the idea phase generally starts with an *assessment of the current situation*: establishing the general status quo at the enterprise, comparing objectives with progress, gaining an understanding of the industry environment, and evaluating relevant environmental conditions. This very early stage of the project is when the core team is put together (*team set-up*).

Business concept development proper starts with a—usually vague—notion of the overall *objective* to be pursued and an *idea*, more specifically a business idea, or the search for such an idea.[1] Apart from the occasional spontaneous or chance inspiration, business ideas are usually produced through systematic application of creativity techniques. For those on a quest for visionary business ideas, the driving incentive is to recognize, now, potential that no one else has yet discovered. The challenge is therefore to describe the markets of the future (cf. Wolf and Hänchen 2012, p. 52). Of course, business ideas need not necessarily be groundbreaking innovations to be worthy of a business model. Substantial improvements and innovative modifications to existing business can also be the trigger and basis for business models.

Creativity techniques—the best-known methods include brainstorming, mind mapping, method 635, bionics and morphological boxes—frequently produce multiple proposals for potential business ideas. Unquestionably, it is simply not economic to examine each and every one of these ideas in detail. The next step is therefore an *evaluation* of all preliminary ideas on the table so far. In the iOcTen Integrated Business Model, this preliminary evaluation is conducted in two stages. The usefulness and feasibility of the idea in principle are explored—at this early stage fairly briefly—first on the basis of *decision-making scope* and then with the core *normative framework* element. In the light of the key role of value and the value proposition in the ultimate success of a business model, the ideas are then examined in terms of their benefits for customers and business partners (core element: *value*).

At the end of the idea phase, a provisional *rough concept* for the planned business is drafted, primarily using the elements *normative framework, value* and *strategy*. The next *steps* in developing the business concept are also *roughly planned* to move forward from this early stage of the project.

Phase II: Analysis

Once the idea has undergone initial evaluation and a rough concept has been drafted, the analysis phase then evaluates in depth those aspects which are essential to realization of the business idea.

The main focus at the start of the analysis phase is to *understand* the concerns and interests of potential *customers* or *business partners* and to draw the necessary conclusions (core element: *customer*). Assumptions on value from the idea

---

[1] This aspect is represented in the Integrated Business Model by the 'idea' component.

phase, so far only preliminary, are now also explored and specified in detail (core element: *value*).

A subsequent *environmental analysis* returns to the findings on decision-making scope reached in the idea phase and explores these in more detail. Relevant industry and market parameters are then analyzed in depth using the core element *market*. A range of professional market research methods and sources are used in this *market analysis*, for example databases, primary and secondary studies, and information from associations and public authorities. Such extensive research should build up a strong understanding of the target markets in question (cf. Wolf and Hänchen 2012, p. 53).

If an idea is to lead to a useful business concept and ultimately to a business model, decision-makers must be absolutely clear about the *skills* and *resources* available within their enterprise and network (core elements: *enablers, partners* and *finance*). Without an objective assessment of the enterprise's economic and technical options, there is a serious danger of business concept implementation failing due to a lack of resources.

On the basis of data from the idea phase and their understanding of the enterprise's abilities, decision-makers then *evaluate the need for action* before *pinpointing the critical success factors* for the business model.

An initial *assessment of potential* for the business idea or the later business model is conducted on the basis of an analysis of the customer, value, environment, market and need for action aspects. At this point at the latest, the management must critically examine the idea in the light of economic considerations (core element: *revenue*). In business practice, this is not infrequently the point at which a new business idea is abandoned.

Phase III: Design

The design phase draws on the findings of the two preceding phases, idea and analysis. Various conceivable *options* are *established* and carefully examined. As outlined in Sect. 3.4, success factors operate together with 'need for action': possible options can be pinpointed by applying and considering the factors for success.

Once the options for business action are known and the results of the idea and analysis phase have been processed, one or more detailed concepts are drafted or *prototypes designed*. This involves designing the processes required for output (core element: *processes*) and defining suitable forms of cooperation (core element: *partners*).

Prototypes should then be *tested* extensively, if possible in real market conditions or failing that in the laboratory. These tests are extremely important, as they can uncover any problems with the idea at an early stage. Should significant flaws in the concept emerge during prototyping, alternative solutions must be found or in some cases even new business concepts developed. In these cases, an enterprise must return to start of the development process.

Prototyping ends with the *selection* of the best overall solution. At this point in business concept development, however, the four core elements *enablers, processes, partners* and *finance* have yet to be evaluated in depth. Using these four elements, the enterprise now *specifies in detail* just how the business concept is to create value. These findings, together with data from the remaining six core objects, are the basis for subsequent design work.

Following prototyping, management reaches a final decision on which of the business concepts developed are to be implemented. A business plan is drawn up for the most promising development paths or prototypes; business plans provide a detailed cost-benefit analysis for business models and can uncover possible weaknesses (cf. Wirtz 2011, p. 235 f.). A *business plan* is also the main planning tool for later business model implementation. Business plans contain information on the human, material and time resources required for introducing and operating a business model.

Each completed business plan is checked against findings from the ten core elements to pick up on any conflicts or contradictions that may still exist, and to uncover and address any logical inconsistencies. On the basis of the fully developed business plans, management then *decides* which of the business concepts or detailed concepts developed is to be translated into a business model and implemented. The final step in the design phase is therefore management's decision whether to implement the business concept in the planned form, or to modify it, or to abandon implementation entirely (cf. Doleski 2012, p. 140).

4.2 Introducing Business Models

Now that the business concept has been drafted, the second stage of *business model development* is actual implementation in business practice. Section 2.2 introduced the distinction between a business concept that has yet to be implemented and a business model that is already in place. As the concept has now been realized, the following paragraphs refer to the "business model".

Phase IV: Implementation

Rough implementation planning was part of the idea phase, and detailed concepts were developed in the design phase. Now comes planning in detail on the basis of this data. The aim of *detailed planning* is to develop as accurate as possible a picture of the best possible implementation procedure for the business model. This aspect of business model introduction therefore includes a precise definition of all critical activities in the implementation project, and the production of a realistic project plan. Each plan consists of multiple, coordinated aspects including at the least the following planning modules: structural, activity, schedule, milestone and resource planning (cf. Doleski and Janner 2013, p. 115).

Following implementation planning, the *implementation team* is *formed* and officially *installed*. Unlike the core team established in Phase I, this is the business model development team responsible for operational implementation.

Once detailed planning is complete, the *organization* must *inform* its internal and external stakeholders about the upcoming implementation of the new business model. A suitable, target group-specific communication strategy is required that responds as effectively as possible to all the interests of the various stakeholders or others affected by the project. Communication relating to business model introduction is therefore aimed at staff, managers, owners, customers, network partners and where applicable also at selected representatives of the business sector and of the public. Communication is designed not just for a general announcement of the new business; it should also explain the objectives and approach of the new implementation project. Early communication helps to increase acceptance of the business model both amongst internal organization staff and on the part of customers and the value creation partners involved (cf. Wirtz 2011, p. 259). A well-structured information campaign through a range of channels counters the 'fear of the new' that is often encountered amongst staff in particular (cf. Osterwalder and Pigneur 2011, p. 261).

Staff training is also recommended as an accompanying measure, either prior to or in parallel to business model introduction.

The new *business model* is then finally *introduced* in accordance with the detailed planning undertaken at the start of this phase. All findings from all core elements in the Integrated Business Model gathered in the previous phases are considered and implemented in accordance with the proposed integrative approach.

The process of business model introduction ends with implementation of the new business. Ideally, however, project performance is evaluated and the main findings of the design and implementation process are first recorded in a final report; this stage of *project completion* comes before the *final handover*. The final report sets out the *lessons learned* and is of direct use in subsequent business model initiatives (cf. Doleski 2012, p. 141).

4.3 Developing Business Models

As outlined at the beginning, even established products and services that have been bringing an enterprise a steady yield with high margins for decades can come under pressure due to changing conditions, increasing competition, technological developments, etc. Modern management cannot content itself with merely reacting to these changes. Business opportunities often lie in a combination of great industry expertise and experience, and innovative ideas for the relevant business environment of the future. 'Yesterday is the seeds of today, and today decides tomorrow'[2] (Bleicher 2011, p. 74). To carry this approach to its logical conclusion, the survival of existing business models—not just the development of wholly new business concepts—can be secured through systematic further development.

Phase V: Improvement

Enterprises must continuously *evaluate* their existing *business models*. All strengths and weaknesses of established product and service portfolios should be monitored on an ongoing basis in the light of dynamic environmental conditions: this gives enterprises a useful indication of the continuing viability of their portfolio. Monitoring and evaluation processes draw on the ten core elements of the iOcTen Integrated Business Model (cf. Wirtz 2011, p. 288).

If a routine evaluation of an established business model finds that the existing business no longer meets the demands of the relevant market and therefore requires modification, this sparks the *development of ideas* for steps ranging from evolutionary development to complete and radical overhaul. Practical implementation of the ideas developed follows the procedure in Phase I 'Idea'.

Business success depends on a range of factors, one of which is an organization's ability rapidly to adapt to changing conditions and thus secure its economic survival. Yet to adapt to new conditions, an enterprise must follow the evaluation of its business model with a precise *analysis* of the relevant *environment* for its business activities and draw the necessary conclusions (Phase II: 'Analysis'). Ultimately, changes ranging from minor modifications to major upheavals in the external business environment are the main triggers for change to established business models.

Now that an idea for business model innovation stands, the *improved business model* can be *designed*. As for re-evaluation of the original business model, the ten

---

[2] *Das Gestrige ist die Wurzel des Heutigen und dies wiederum entscheidet über das Morgen.*

core elements of iOcTen are also used to develop a new, viable business model. As this step in practice follows the procedure in Phase III, 'Design', it usually involves drafting and testing at least one prototype and a subsequent decision-making phase.

Once management has agreed in principle on the implementation of the business model innovation, i.e. has decided either to develop or completely overhaul the original business model, the *model* can then be *introduced* and subsequently *operated*.

A special case of improvement is *business model extension*: the application of a business model to new markets and/or regions in order significantly to extend the reach of existing business.

Shaping the Future: From Driven To Driver

5

The iOcTen Integrated Business Model introduced here is designed to help enterprises shape their economic future by providing decision-makers, strategists and organizational developers with a useful, practical tool for implementing business model development initiatives. The main benefits offered by iOcTen are as follows:

- **Open architecture**
  The Integrated Business Model is a universal approach that is open and integrative in design. It does not limit the user to specific businesses or specific aspects of the value chain.
- **Interdisciplinarity**
  Findings and factors from system and decision theory, economics, engineering, psychology and a range of other disciplines have all gone into the development of this comprehensive business model.
- **Completeness**
  Together, the various elements of the model cover in full the normative, strategic and operational dimensions of management. This minimizes the risk of important content being forgotten, and of seemingly unimportant aspects carelessly being ignored in business model design: nothing important is forgotten, and nothing is ignored.
- **Managing complexity**
  The Integrated Business Model allows enterprises to manage complexity by systematically considering all relevant conditions and influencing factors. Instead of simply ignoring complexity, this model splits it up into separate and manageable aspects.

© Springer Fachmedien Wiesbaden 2015
O. D. Doleski, *Integrated Business Model*, essentials,
DOI 10.1007/978-3-658-09698-4_5

- **Communication focus**
  The integrated approach considers the expectations of relevant stakeholders and is therefore fundamentally communication-focused.
- **Selection and gatekeeper function**
  The structured process flags up possible weaknesses in the planned business model at an early stage. Decision-makers can therefore decide before wasting time and resources whether changes are necessary and possible, or whether the project should in fact be abandoned. This avoids the risk of spiraling non-value costs from the business model development stage.

One of the keys to business success lies in optimized market propositions. In an increasingly complex environment, business models now more than ever require comprehensive design and structured implementation if they are to achieve long-term success. Ideally, standardized business development methods should be used. The many benefits associated with the Integrated Business Model presented here should firmly recommend it to the reader. iOcTen can help enterprises to retain or regain the economic initiative. The systematic design of sustainable business models is without a doubt the main opportunity for all enterprises, regardless of their size or sector, to take their development into their own hands and become the drivers of tomorrow.

What this 'Essential' offers

- Help in shaping business options with an integrative approach to business models
- The basics of a useful, practical tool for implementing business model innovation initiatives
- A structured guide to systematic development of new business ideas in complex business environments
- A step-by-step procedure for adapting and developing existing business models

© Springer Fachmedien Wiesbaden 2015
O. D. Doleski, *Integrated Business Model*, essentials,
DOI 10.1007/978-3-658-09698-4

References

Bach, N.: Vernetzung als strategische Option in der deutschen Leiterplattenindustrie. In: Bach, N., Buchholz, W., Eichler, B. (eds.) Geschäftsmodelle für Wertschöpfungsnetzwerke, pp. 331–345. Gabler, Wiesbaden (2003)

Bach, N., Buchholz, W., Eichler, B.: Geschäftsmodelle für Wertschöpfungsnetzwerke—Begriffliche und konzeptionelle Grundlagen. In: Bach, N., Buchholz, W., Eichler, B. (eds.) Geschäftsmodelle für Wertschöpfungsnetzwerke, pp. 1–20. Gabler, Wiesbaden (2003)

Becker, W., et al.: Geschäftsmodelle im Mittelstand, Bamberger Betriebswirtschaftliche Beiträge No. 175, Bamberg (2011)

Becker, W., et al.: Erfolgsfaktoren der Geschäftsmodelle junger Unternehmen, Bamberger Betriebswirtschaftliche Beiträge No. 183, Bamberg (2012)

Bergmann, R., Bungert, M.: Strategische Unternehmensführung, 2nd edn, Springer, Berlin (2011)

Bleicher, K.: Integriertes Management von Wertschöpfungsnetzwerken. In: Bach, N., Buchholz, W., Eichler, B. (eds.) Geschäftsmodelle für Wertschöpfungsnetzwerke, pp. 145–178. Gabler, Wiesbaden (2003)

Bleicher, K.: Das Konzept Integriertes Management. Visionen—Missionen—Programme, 8th edn, Campus, Frankfurt a. M. (2011)

Bornemann, M.: Die Erfolgswirkung der Geschäftsmodellgestaltung—Eine kontextabhängige Betrachtung. Gabler, Wiesbaden (2010)

Bühner, V., et al.: Neue Dienstleistungen und Geschäftsmodelle für Smart Distribution und Smart Markets, VDE-Kongress 2012. VDE-Verlag, Berlin (2012)

Doleski, O.D.: Geschäftsprozesse der liberalisierten Energiewirtschaft. In: Aichele, C. (ed.) Smart Energy—Von der reaktiven Kundenverwaltung zum proaktiven Kundenmanagement, pp. 115–150. Springer Vieweg, Wiesbaden (2012)

Doleski, O.D., Janner, T.: Projektmanagement bei der Ausbringung intelligenter Zähler. In: Aichele, C., Doleski, O.D. (eds.) Smart Meter Rollout—Praxisleitfaden zur Ausbringung intelligenter Zähler, pp. 105–129. Springer Vieweg, Wiesbaden (2013)

Gutenberg, E.: Einführung in die Betriebswirtschaftslehre, Gabler, Wiesbaden, 1st edn, unveränd. Nachdruck (1990)

Hahn, H., Prinz, M.: Szenariotechnik als Instrument der Strategieentwicklung. Z. Energ. Markt. Wettbew. (emw). **2**, 46–49 (2013)

Kley, F.: Neue Geschäftsmodelle zur Ladeinfrastruktur, working paper sustainability and innovation No. S 5/2011, Fraunhofer-Institut für System- und Innovationsforschung ISI, Karlsruhe (2011)

Nemeth, A.: Geschäftsmodellinnovation—Theorie und Praxis der erfolgreichen Realisierung von strategischen Innovationen in Großunternehmen. Dissertation, St. Gallen (2011)

Osterwalder, A.: The business model ontology. A proposition in a design science approach. Dissertation, Universität Lausanne (2004)

Osterwalder, A., Pigneur, Y.: Business model generation. Campus, Frankfurt a. M. (2011)

Osterwalder, A., et al.: Clarifying business models: origins, present, and future of the concept. Commun. Assoc. Inf. Syst. (CAIS). **15**, 1–39 (2005). (Nachdruck)

Porter, M.E.: Strategy and the Internet. Harv. Bus. Rev. **79**, 62–78 (2001)

Rüegg-Stürm, J.: Das neue St. Galler Management-Modell. In: Dubs, R. et al. (eds.): Einführung in die Managementlehre, vol. 1, pp. 65–141. Haupt, Bern (2004). (section A–E)

Scheer, Ch., et al.: Geschäftsmodelle und internetbasierte Geschäftsmodelle—Begriffsbestimmung und Teilnehmermodell, ISYM, Paper 12, Dezember (2003)

Stähler, P.: Geschäftsmodelle in der digitalen Ökonomie, 2nd edn, Eul, Lohmar (2002)

Weiner, N., et al.: Geschäftsmodelle im „Internet der Dienste"—Aktueller Stand in Forschung und Praxis. Fraunhofer-Institut für Arbeitswirtschaft und Organisation IAO, Stuttgart (2010)

Wirtz, B.W.: Business Model Management. Design—Instrumente—Erfolgsfaktoren von Geschäftsmodellen, 2nd edn, Gabler, Wiesbaden (2011)

Wolf, T., Hänchen, S.: Die Entwicklung visionärer Geschäftsmodelle. Fachz. Inf. Manage. Consult. (IM). **4**, 50–56 (2012)

Zolnowski, A., Böhmann, T.: Stand und Perspektiven der Modellierung von Geschäftsmodellen aus Sicht des Dienstleistungsmanagements. In: Thomas, O., Nüttgens, M. (eds.) Dienstleistungsmodellierung 2010, pp. 24–38. Springer, Berlin (2010)